Draw with

ART FOR KIDS HUB

CUTE & FUNNY
FOODS

30 step-by-step drawing projects inside!

Rob Jensen

Senior Designer Lauren Adams
Senior Production Editor Jennifer Murray
Senior Production Controller Louise Minihane
Senior Acquisitions Editor Pete Jorgensen
Managing Art Editor Jo Connor
Managing Director Mark Searle
Written and Illustrated by Rob Jensen

Designed and Edited by Elizabeth T. Gilbert and Rebecca Razo
at Coffee Cup Creative, LLC.

Copyedited by Beth Adelman

First American Edition, 2024
Published in the United States by DK Publishing
1745 Broadway, 20th Floor, New York, NY 10019

Page design copyright © 2024 Dorling Kindersley Limited
DK, a Division of Penguin Random House LLC
24 25 26 27 28 10 9 8 7 6 5 4 3 2 1
001–339832–July/2024

© 2024 Art for Kids Hub

A catalog record for this book
is available from the Library of Congress.
ISBN 978-0-7440-9898-3

DK books are available at special discounts when purchased
in bulk for sales promotions, premiums, fund-raising, or educational use.
For details, contact: DK Publishing Special Markets,
1745 Broadway, 20th Floor, New York, NY 10019
SpecialSales@dk.com

Printed and bound in China

www.dk.com

www.artforkidshub.com

This book was made with Forest
Stewardship Council™ certified
paper – one small step in DK's
commitment to a sustainable future.
**Learn more at www.dk.com/uk/
information/sustainability**

Draw with ART FOR KIDS HUB

CUTE & FUNNY FOODS

30 step-by-step drawing projects inside!

Rob Jensen

DK

PART I: Step-by-Step Projects....16

Table of CONTENTS

PART II: You're an Artist!....78

Welcome to  Art for Kids Hub!

Hey, friends! I'm Rob. And along with my amazing wife, Teryn, and our four creative kids, Jack, Hadley, Austin, and Olivia, we make art together as a family— and we love sharing it with you!

This book is divided into two parts. In Part I, you'll find step-by-step drawing lessons for a variety of cute and funny foods! Each drawing is ranked Level 1, Level 2, or Level 3 according to its difficulty (see the Symbol Key on the opposite page). Don't worry, though! You'll be able to draw all the projects by following along step by step.

In Part II, you'll find tips for drawing backgrounds, props, and completed scenes. I've also included some folding surprise drawing projects at the very end. Whether you're a beginner or a budding artist, there's something fun for everyone.

Ready to begin? Grab your art tools and some paper, and let's make art that brings smiles and creates joy!

ROB

TERYN

AUSTIN

JACK

OLIVIA

HADLEY

About This Book

For each project, follow the steps in red to complete your drawing. Then add color using your favorite art tools. It's as simple as that!

1

2

3

Symbol Key

Each project is marked with one of the following symbols, from less difficult to a little more challenging. But don't be afraid to try them all!

 = Level 1

 = Level 2

 = Level 3

 = Great work!

MORE IN THIS BOOK

☑ Draw spoons, forks, and other food-related props.

☑ Combine drawings to make completed scenes.

☑ Create fun folding surprise drawings.

Art Tools & SUPPLIES

Here are some art tools you can use to draw and color the projects in this book. These are some of my favorite supplies, but you can use any tools that are available to you.

Black Marker

I like to draw with a permanent black marker for a bold, solid outline. But feel free to begin your drawings with pencil if you prefer.

CHECKLIST

☑ A flat drawing surface, like a table or clipboard

☑ Marker paper

☑ Black permanent marker

☑ Pencil and sharpener

☑ Coloring tools, such as colored pencils, markers, and crayons

Paper

White marker paper is perfect if you're using markers to color, and regular paper is fine if you are using crayons or colored pencils.

Markers

Markers create smooth, solid strokes of color. Some sets include both fine tips and thick tips. I use alcohol-based markers because they dry quickly, and their colors don't fade easily.

Crayons

Wax crayons are inexpensive and easy to find. Sometimes they create a bumpy texture and can be hard to blend, so I use gel crayons. They are creamy and extra smooth.

Colored Pencils

These tools are clean and simple. You can even layer them to blend and shade. Keep a sharpener on hand for pointy tips.

Pastels

There are two types of pastels: soft pastels and oil pastels. Soft pastels feel like chalk and create smooth, light blends. Oil pastels feel more like crayons and create bold, bright strokes.

We would LOVE to see your drawings! Learn how to share them with us here.

Brushes

Brushes come in a range of sizes and shapes. Those with natural bristles are best for watercolor paints, and brushes with synthetic bristles are best for acrylics. When you've finished painting, rinse your brushes with soap and warm water, and reshape the bristles before they dry.

Paints

Watercolor, tempera, and acrylic are water-based paints that you can use to color your art. Be sure to use them on sturdy paper, such as watercolor paper. While you paint, keep a cup of water nearby for rinsing your brushes—and have plenty of paper towels on hand for cleanup.

WATERCOLOR

TEMPERA

ACRYLIC

Getting STARTED

Before you begin drawing, it's a great idea to warm up. From dots and swirls to dashes and curls, make all sorts of marks on scrap paper to get the creative juices flowing.

I use a lot of loops, dots, and curvy, squiggly, and jagged lines in my drawings. What other lines and scribbles can you make?

Basic Shapes

Most of the drawings in the book start with basic shapes like circles, triangles, squares, and ovals. Practice drawing these basic shapes and then draw new shapes of your own, if you like.

TRIANGLES

SQUARES, RECTANGLES & DIAMONDS

CIRCLES, OVALS & BEAN SHAPES

A happy expression is my favorite, but it's fun to draw other emotions too.

Expressions

The face reveals a character's emotions. In the examples below, see how the eyes, mouth, and other features can help you communicate feelings and personality.

HAPPY

SCARED

SILLY

ANGRY

SNEAKY

TIRED

EMBARRASSED

SWEET

EXCITED

All About COLOR

The Color Wheel

The color wheel is a visual aid for understanding how colors work together. The colors on this wheel are divided into two groups: primary (blue, yellow, red) and secondary (green, orange, purple).

Complementary Colors

Complementary colors are two colors that are opposite each other on the color wheel. When they're placed next to each other in a drawing or painting, they appear brighter. Some examples are yellow and purple, blue and orange, and red and green.

Color Temperature

Colors are divided into two temperatures: cool and warm. Blue, green, and purple are cool colors. Yellow, orange, and red are warm colors. Color temperature plays a part in the mood of a drawing. For example, cool colors are calm and warm colors are energetic.

WARM

COOL

Color Mixing

Every color combination begins with the primary colors. Secondary colors are made by mixing two primary colors. Yellow + red = orange, red + blue = purple, and blue + yellow = green. Gray is made by mixing white and black, while pink is made from a combination of white and red. White lightens colors; black darkens colors.

Coloring Steps

To bring your characters to life, try this three-step approach to adding color.

Add smooth, flat areas of color with your tools of choice.

Layer your colors—or use slightly darker shades—to create shadows.

Finish coloring your art by adding highlights with white.

I like to get creative with color in my drawings! How about you?

Part I: STEP-BY-STEP PROJECTS

Hey, art friends!

To draw the cute and funny foods in this section, start with step 1 and continue to follow each new step in red. Along the way, you'll find lots of encouragement, helpful art tips, and even some fun and interesting facts.

I had so much fun creating these drawing lessons, but we especially love drawing together as a family. So, in addition to my drawings, you'll also see tons of great drawings by Teryn, Jack, Hadley, Austin, and Olivia. Each of us has our own art style, and we want to inspire you to draw in your own unique style, too. There are no mistakes and no wrong ways to make art—the important thing is to have fun and practice!

Happy creating!

Hank the HOT DOG

Begin the bun and draw the eyes.

1

2

Now add the hot dog, the rest of the bun, and the mouth.

3

4

Draw the tongue and your toppings.

5

Try This!

19

DeeDee the UNI-DONUT

3

Draw the bow and begin the hair.

1

2

3

Continue to follow the steps in red.

4

5

6

Add the ears and horn.

7

8

Try This!

Turn back to page 13 and select another expression for your uni-donut.

Draw the icing and sprinkles.

9

Iggy the ICE POP

△ 1

DID YOU KNOW?
The first ice pop was created in 1905 by an 11-year-old named Frank Epperson. Frank accidentally left a stirring stick in a cup of soda on the porch overnight, and it froze. When he pulled on the stick, the frozen soda came out with it and the first ice pop was born!

Draw the shape of the ice pop. Then add the eyes and mouth.

1

2

3

Finish the face. Then add the stick and drip mark.

4

5

Wilma the WAFFLE

Draw a circle and pat of butter. Begin the face and the waffle pattern.

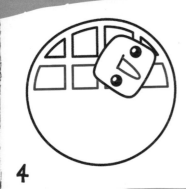

1

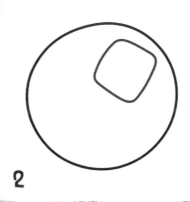

2

3

Continue to follow each new step in red. You're doing great!

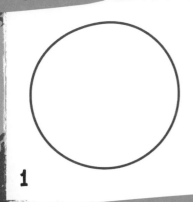

4

5

6

Add a curvy line for the syrup. Yum!

7

Egg & Bacon BESTIES

Begin with wavy lines to start the egg and bacon. Draw the yolk and eyes.

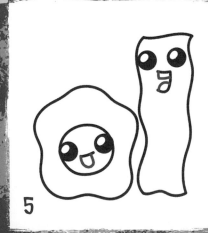

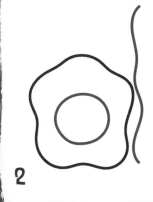

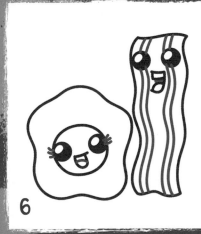

Continue to add the details.

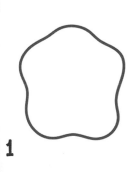

Looks great!

Try This!

Follow Austin's lead and add some cool elements to your drawing, like a frying pan or salt and pepper shakers. Turn to page 81 for some ideas.

Monty the MEATBALL MONSTER

Draw a wobbly circle. Add the eyes, sauce drips, and tiny loops for the first pasta noodle.

1

2

3

Draw the mouth and continue the spaghetti loops.

4

5

6

Continue drawing the spaghetti loops. Then add the fork and basil leaves.

7

8

9

Begin with a dome shape for the top of the bun. Start the face.

1

2

3

Complete the face. Add sesame seeds and start the fillings.

4

5

6

Continue to draw the details and add the burger patty.

7

8

9

Draw the bottom bun. That's a great cheeseburger!

10

Try This!

Want to make your burger extra tall? Continue to draw more fillings and extra patties before drawing the bottom bun.

Happy the HOT CHOCOLATE

Want to add whipped cream to your hot chocolate? Draw a puffy cloud over the mouth of the cup and then add the marshmallows on top.

Turn to page 70 to see how to draw whipped cream.

Draw an oval. Add eyes and a U shape for the cup.

1

2

Continue to follow the steps in red.

3

4

Add another marshmallow. Finish the mouth and handle.

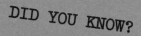

5

6

Draw the faces and the heat swirl.

7

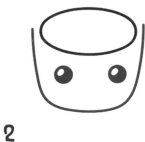

Sammy the SANDWICH

Draw the top of a heart connected to a rectangle. Add eyes.

1

2

3

Outline the bread. Add a mouth and some fillings.

4

5

6

Continue to follow the steps in red to complete the drawing.

7

8

My sandwich hasn't lost all its baby teeth yet.

DID YOU KNOW?

The first sandwich was created in 1762 at the request of John Montagu, 4th Earl of Sandwich. He asked a cook to prepare a food that he could eat when he wasn't at the dinner table. The cook returned with pieces of meat placed between two slices of toasted bread.

I gave my sandwich a bow, eyelashes, and a cute smile.

35

Penelope PANCAKES

Draw an oval. Add the eyes and nose.

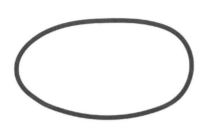

1

2

Finish the nose and mouth. Begin the next pancake.

3

4

Draw the final pancake and begin the plate.

5

6

Finish the details to complete the stack.

7

I love all the extras you added to your drawing, Olivia!

Thanks, Dad. I wanted mine to have arms and hands.

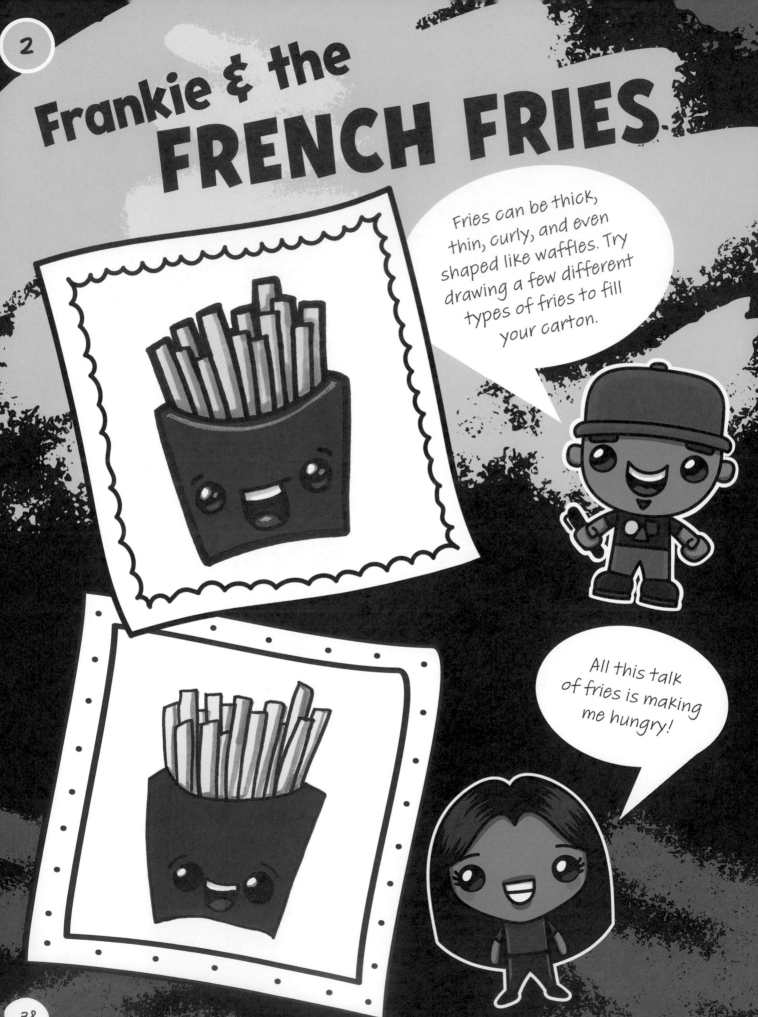

Draw the carton using a few simple lines.

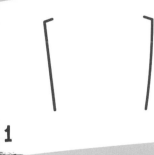

1

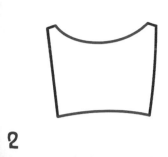

2

Add a few fries, and then begin the face.

3

4

Continue drawing the mouth and more fries.

5

6

Finish the details. Great job!

7

DID YOU KNOW?

French fries aren't from France! That's because the name doesn't describe where they're from, but rather how they are prepared— by "Frenching," a way of cutting an ingredient so it cooks evenly on all sides.

Frosty the FRO-YO

3

DID YOU KNOW?

Fro-yo, or frozen yogurt, was originally nicknamed "fro-gurt" when it was introduced in the 1970s as a soft-serve treat. Although some fro-yo contains ingredients similar to store-bought yogurt, it is more of a treat, like ice cream, than a healthy snack.

Begin the cup and the swirl.

1

2

3

Keep drawing the swirl. Add some sweet toppings.

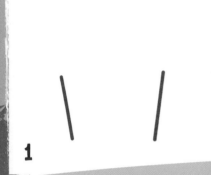

4

5

6

Now add more swirl lines. Draw the eyes, mouth, and spoon.

7

8

9

40

Finish the details. Well done!

10

Try This!

What's the best fro-yo you've ever had in your life? Draw it now. Don't forget to add all your favorite toppings.

I drew vanilla and chocolate with candy. What kind did you draw?

Mine is raspberry and vanilla swirl with blueberries, strawberries, and gummy candy.

Soosh & Hee SUSHI ROLLS

2

DID YOU KNOW?

The dark green paperlike wrap on sushi rolls is an edible type of seaweed called nori.

Draw three connected lines and an oval. Draw a partial cloud shape for the rice.

1

2

Continue to follow the steps in red to add the details. Draw the eyes.

3

4

Finish the details. Excellent!

5

We drew nigiri and maki sushi. Nigiri is a small slice of fish on top of rice. Maki is a roll that includes rice and other ingredients wrapped in seaweed.

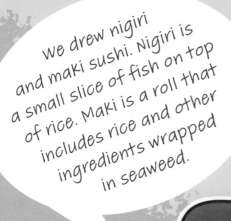

These are two very happy sushi rolls!

Try This!

Sushi comes in a variety of shapes, sizes, and ingredients. Draw some different sushi rolls, making them as wild, colorful, and creative as you like.

Tommy the TACO

Follow the steps in red to begin the shell and some fillings.

1

2

Complete the shell, add some more fillings, and begin the face.

3

4

5

Complete the details.

6

7

When you add unexpected elements to your drawings, the artwork becomes uniquely personal to you.

I like adding details that make my drawings extra fun.

Try This!

Add one or two elements to your taco that reflect your personality. Are you a skater? Give your taco a skateboard! Do you surf, swim, or practice martial arts? The ideas are endless!

Tony-roni PIZZA SLICE

DID YOU KNOW?
Pizza hails from Naples, Italy, where it was created in the 19th century as an inexpensive and convenient meal that could be eaten quickly.

I love deep dish pepperoni pizza. How about you?

I call my drawing the "Leaning Tower of Pizza!" I gave my slice arms and legs to help it balance.

Use simple lines to begin the pizza slice.

1

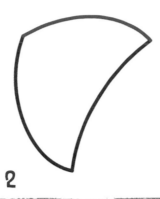

2

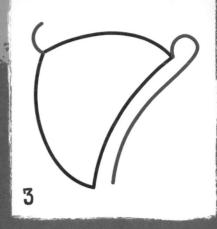

3

Continue to add the details, and begin the face.

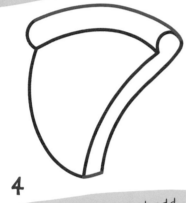

4

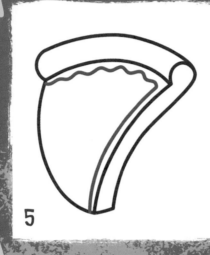

5

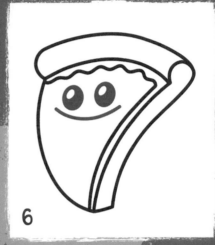

6

Complete the face and add the pepperoni.

7

8

What are your favorite pizza toppings? Add those to your slice—or draw the entire pie!

Try This!

Polly the PINEAPPLE

Draw an oval. Begin the stem.

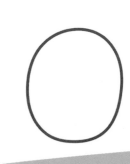

1

2

3

Continue adding leaves to finish the stem. Draw the face.

4

5

6

Draw criss-cross lines to create the pattern.

7

8

Coco the CANDY BAR

Draw a partial square and a jagged line. Then draw the top of the wrapper.

1

2
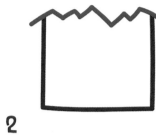

3

Draw the eyes, mouth, eyebrows, and other details.

4

5

6

Add a bite mark and rectangles to the candy bar. Looks great!

7

8

Chad & Cheryl CHERRY CHUMS

Draw the first cherry and begin the second cherry.

1

2

3

Finish the second cherry. Then draw the stems, eyes, and a leaf.

4

5

6

Add the finishing touches. Great work!

7

8

Begin with geometric lines to create the basic shape.

1

2

3

Finish the candy top, and then begin the ring. Draw the eyes.

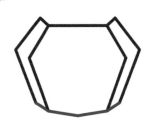

4

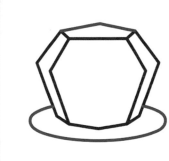

5

6

Draw the smile and eyelashes, and finish the details.

7

8

Try This!

To give your ring a bit of sparkle, use a glittery gel pen in your favorite color.

Big Pop POPCORN

I love extra buttery popcorn. What kind of popcorn do you like?

Drawing popcorn is like drawing little clouds.

Draw the bag base. Add a zigzag line across the top and a piece of popcorn.

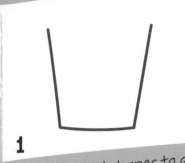

1

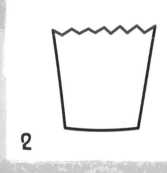

2

3

Draw little cloud shapes to add more popcorn to the bag.

4

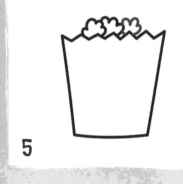

5

6

Continue to fill the bag with popcorn. Begin the face.

7

8

9

Finish the details. Hooray!

10

Try This!

For extra fun, draw faces on all the popcorn pieces in the bag.

Wally the WATERMELON

Draw a wedge shape with a little bite mark.

1

2

Finish the top edge, and then add the face and rind.

3

4

Draw the watermelon's seeds and tongue.

5

Be sure to add extras to your drawing! I added a heart.

I gave my watermelon slice a party hat and dancing legs.

Try This!

In the real world, watermelon is red on the inside and green on the outside. But in the cartoon world, it can be any color you like, so feel free to get creative.

Begin with two perpendicular lines, and follow the steps in red.

1

2

3

Continue to draw the shape of the pretzel, following the steps.

4

5

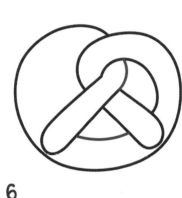
6

Draw the face, salt, and final details.

7

8

Do you like to dip your pretzels in cheese or mustard? Add one or both to your drawing!

Try This!

Bobby the BOBA TEA

Draw the cup and rim. Add silly eyes.

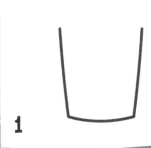

1

2

3

Add a dome-shaped lid and a wavy line for the liquid. Don't forget the straw.

4

5

6

Finish the details. Great job!

7

8

Cloud the COTTON CANDY

Draw a puffy cloud shape. Begin the face.

1

2

3

Draw the paper cone and finish the details.

4

5

Drawing cotton candy is fun, don't you think?

It's fun to eat, too!

Try This!

Draw several cotton candy friends, each in a different color and with a different expression. Then cut them out and have a cotton candy party!

Yummy the GUMMY

DID YOU KNOW?

Gummy candy comes in a variety of shapes, sizes, and types. Flavors range from fruity to sweet to sour to red hot. The biggest gummy bear ever weighs nearly 3,810 pounds!

Draw a bunch of gummy bears in different colors and then give each one a different facial expression using the guide on page 13—or add your own!

I'm going to draw an entire bag of gummy bears next.

Try This!

Grab a large poster board and art tools; then draw a giant gummy bear for someone special.

Draw the eyes, head, ears, and nose.

1

2

3

Finish the face. Draw the body and legs.

4

5

6

Complete the details. What a cutie!

7

8

Cutie Pie CUPCAKE

Draw a heart and begin the cupcake outline.

1

2

3

Continue to follow the steps in red.

4

5

6

Don't forget the sprinkles!

7

8

That looks like a yummy chocolate cupcake, Hadley.

What kind of cupcake did you draw?

Try This!

Draw a dozen cupcakes and give each one a different expression, color, and topping. For extra fun, give them all silly names!

Minnie the MILKSHAKE

Begin with a U shape for the cup. Add the rim and begin the whipped cream.

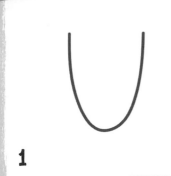

1

2

3

Continue by following the steps in red.

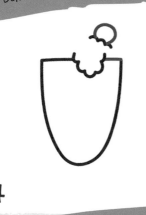

4

5

6

Finish the details. That looks great!

7

8

What is the craziest milkshake you can think of? Does it have gobs of whipped cream and a dozen cherries, or is it topped with all your favorite candy bars? Draw it now!

Try This!

Scoops the ICE CREAM CONE

DID YOU KNOW?
There are different kinds of ice cream around the world. The Japanese kind is called mochi. In Italy, it's gelato. In Turkey, it's dondurma. Can you think of any others?

Draw a half circle and curvy lines to begin the scoop. Add the eyes and mouth.

1

2

3

Draw the cone and add sprinkles, if you like.

4

5

Olivia, where is your cone flying off to?

It's flying straight into my mouth, Dad!

Try This!

Add another one, two, or ten scoops to your cone! This is your drawing and you can do whatever you want!

Jumpin' JELLYBEAN PARTY

DID YOU KNOW?
The jellybean is a distant relative of Turkish delight: an ancient Mediterranean sweet made from sugar and fruit syrup.

Turn to page 80 to see an "exploding" jellybean. Then draw your own exploding jellybean party in a variety of colors and shapes.

I added confetti to my jellybean party.

Draw the first jellybean.

1

2

3

Add more jellybeans to the party.
Begin the details.

4

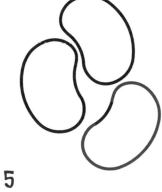

5

6

Finish the faces and party hats.
Now that's a party!

7

8

75

Crumble & Moo
COOKIE & MILK

76

Draw a glass and a wobbly circle for the cookie. Start the outline of the milk.

1

2

3

Finish the milk line, bow, and faces.

4

5

6

Complete the details.

7

Try This!

Add colorful sprinkles or toppings to your cookie to make it extra sweet.

Part II:
YOU'RE AN ARTIST!

In this section, you'll learn how to draw things that add interest to your art. I've also included instructions for creating two folding surprise drawings. Remember, there are no mistakes—your only goal is to have fun!

Symbols

Symbols can be used to express emotions, feelings, or a state of mind. For example, replacing a character's eyes with hearts suggests they might be thinking about love. Drawing sparkles around a birthday cake gives it a festive feel. What other symbols could you add to your drawings?

BIG BOOM!
Use a big boom to show an explosion of thought, action, or excitement!

SPARKLES & HEARTS
Use sparkles to show something magical or festive. Hearts are great for showing affection and emphasizing cute things.

STARS & DIZZY LINES
Did your character bump their head? Use stars and dizzy lines to show confusion.

Speech Bubbles

Add personality to your characters with speech bubbles that show what they're saying or thinking.

Round and rectangular speech bubbles give your characters the ability to "talk" to each other or your readers.

This speech bubble is used to express enthusiasm or excitement!

This thought cloud reveals a character's internal thoughts to the reader.

What Olivia said.

Action & Movement

These fun details can add interest to your food drawings by showing them in action.

EATEN

Bites and scraps show a half-eaten watermelon.

EXPLODING

Jagged lines form a burst to show a jellybean exploding with excitement.

FLOATING

A cloud shape shows a happy hamburger floating in mouthwatering flavor.

MELTING

Long drips, melted splotches, and a surprised expression mean this ice cream cone is melting down fast.

FROZEN

Chattering teeth and icy drips show this fro-yo in a chilly state.

SIZZLING

Call the fire department! This flaming pizza slice is sizzling hot.

Props

Props are things like silverware, tables, chairs, and other objects that add character, style, and a sense of place to your drawings. Turn the page to see some more cool things you can draw and combine to create finished works of art.

CAKE STAND

BISTRO TABLE & CHAIR

FORK, SPOON & KNIFE

SKILLET

FRIDGE

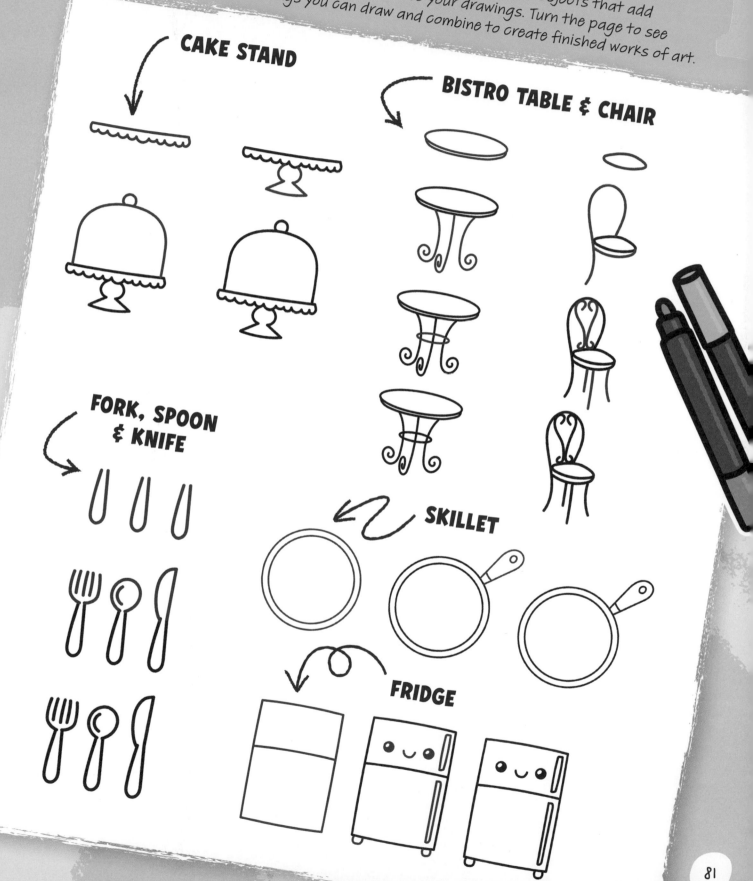

An Eggcellent BREAKFAST!

I love a good breakfast! Here are some props you can draw to accompany your favorite breakfast foods. Turn the page to see the completed breakfast scene I drew. What will you add to your breakfast table?

Butter

Use rectangles and straight lines for a stick of butter.

Carton of Eggs

Ovals and curvy lines work for this eggs-cellent prop!

Maple Syrup

Begin with a bottle shape and draw a face on the label.

Bowl of Fruit

Circles, half-circles, and curvy lines lead to a yummy fruit bowl.

Loaf of Bread

This happy loaf consists of mostly curvy lines.

Hey Teryn, what did the egg say to the bacon?

You're looking very crisp today!

Breakfast, Sunnyside Up

Try This!

Flip back through Part I and select projects that you can put together to create drawings of breakfast, lunch, dinner, and dessert. Don't forget to add fun props to make your artwork stand out!

You two are bacon me crazy!

A Super Cool PICNIC

Once you draw a cooler and a basket, you'll be ready for a picnic at the park or a day at the beach. Turn the page to see my completed scenes.

Cooler

Use rectangles, circles, and curvy lines for this cooler.

Picnic Basket

Draw this basket using simple lines.

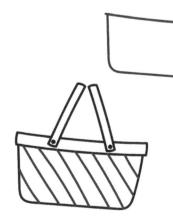

A Picnic to Relish

Life's a Happy Day at the Beach

Sweet Treats TRUCK

Draw an ice cream truck for your sweet, snack-tacular food friends! What treats do you want to add to your truck?

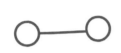

Join lines, circles, squares, and geometric shapes to draw an ice cream truck.

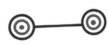

We All Scream for Ice Cream

Folding SURPRISE DRAWINGS

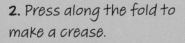

A folding surprise drawing is exactly what it sounds like: a drawing on folded paper that opens to reveal a surprise inside! This project is a lot of fun and gives you an opportunity to stretch your creativity.

Before you begin, you'll need to prepare your paper so the surprise works the way it should. I used a sheet of printer paper (8.5" x 11"), but you can use any size paper you like.

Paper Set Up

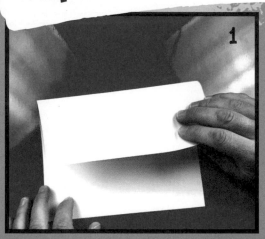

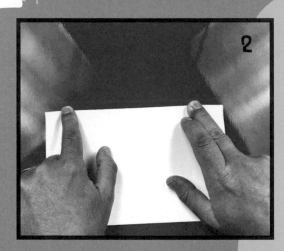

1. Lay the paper flat with the short sides of the paper on the top and bottom, and the long sides of the paper on the left and right. Fold the paper in half, lining up the top edge with the bottom edge.

2. Press along the fold to make a crease.

3. Gently lift the top flap of the paper.

4. Fold the top flap up, bringing the bottom edge to line up with the top edge. Press along the fold to make another crease.

5. and 6. Lift the paper and flip it over from right to left, so that the unfolded bottom flap is now on the top.

7. Lift the flap and fold it up to meet the top edge, repeating step 4.

8. Open the last fold you just made.

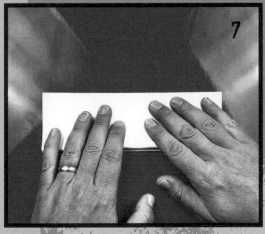

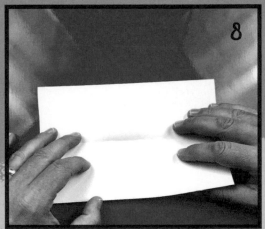

9. Flip your paper over from left to right, so it's back to the original side.

10. Your paper is now ready for your drawing! You will start the outside drawing on the folded paper.

Note: When you unfold the page, you should have four sections marked by folds.

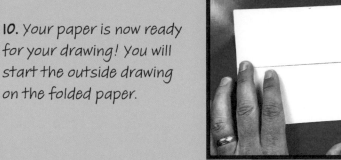

Turn the page to get started on the first surprise drawing!

Four-Scoops ICE CREAM

FOLDED

1. Place the paper with the folded side up (see step 10 on page 89). Draw a semicircle just above the fold line.

2. Draw a squiggly line just below the fold that connects to the semicircle above.

3. Draw the face and the cone.

4. Add the mouth and the eyelashes.

5. Add the drips and the final details.

1
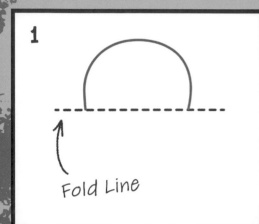
Fold Line

2
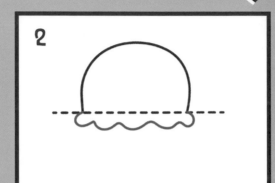

3
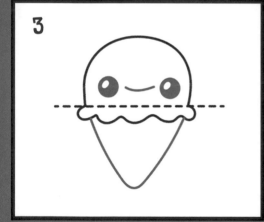

4
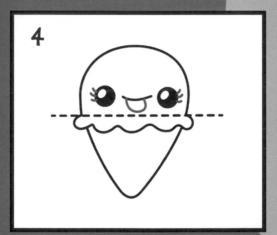

5
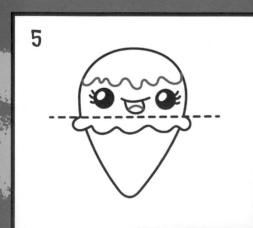

OPENED

1. Unfold your paper. You will see the face above the top fold and the cone below the bottom fold.

2. Draw a squiggly line like the one you drew before, just below the fold line. Draw the next scoop.

3. Add the third and fourth ice cream scoops.

4. Begin drawing the faces.

5. Finish the details.

Turn the page to see how I colored in my four-scoop cone!

1

Top Fold

Bottom Fold

2

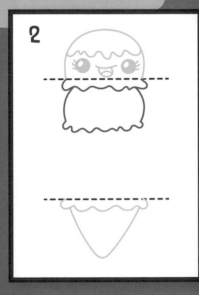

3

4

5

1. Refold the paper so only the outside drawing is visible again. Color your first scoop. I chose a chocolate and vanilla combo that would really make the face stand out. I also added a pattern to the cone.

Try This!

Folding surprise drawings are fun to play with! After you draw and color the Leaning Layers Birthday Cake (see opposite page), create some other cute food folding surprise drawings using the lessons in Part I. Then throw an impromptu party with your new foodie friends!

2. Open the paper. Color the rest of the scoops however you like. Feel free to add sprinkles, candy, hot fudge, or any other colorful toppings.

Leaning Layers **BIRTHDAY CAKE**

3

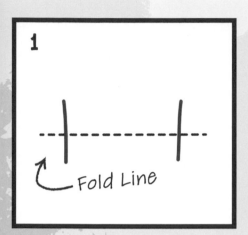

1

Fold Line

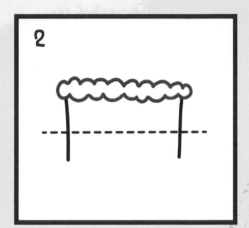

2

3

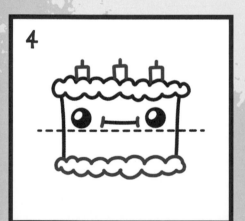

4

5

FOLDED

1. Place the paper with the folded side up (see step 10 on page 89). Draw two vertical parallel lines, evenly spaced, that start above the fold line and finish below the fold line.

2. Draw a long, flattened cloud on top of the parallel lines above the fold.

3. Draw the face just above the fold line.

4. Complete the face. Add candles and another frosting layer, this time at the base of the cake.

5. Light the candles and draw a plate.

You take the cake, my friend!

93

1

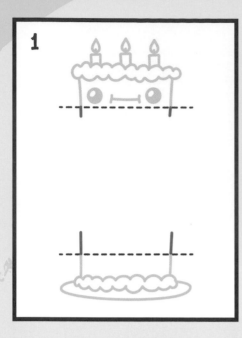

2

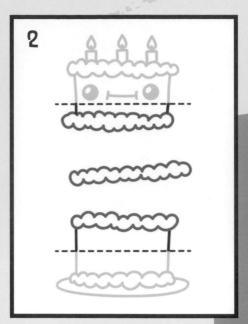

3

4

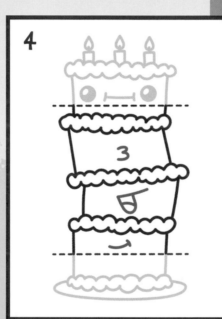

5

OPENED

1. Draw two little parallel lines connected to the top cake, just below the fold line. Draw two more lines above the bottom fold that connect to the cake below.

2. Draw three more flat clouds at slightly wonky angles.

3. Connect each frosting cloud with leaning lines to create two more cake layers.

4. Begin adding the faces.

5. Complete the details.

Try This!

Create expressions different than the ones shown here, if you like!

ABOUT THE ARTIST

Rob Jensen, the fun-loving creator of Art for Kids Hub, has a background in industrial design, which fuels his passion for teaching art. He believes that creativity adds happiness and interest to life. Rob, along with his family, embodies the spirit of making art both easy and exciting. Collectively, the Jensens demonstrate that art is not just a solo journey but a shared family adventure. Together, they show the world how to create art in simple, engaging ways, one drawing at a time.

ABOUT ART FOR KIDS HUB

Art for Kids Hub is a family driven platform that brings the joy of art to families around the world. Co-created by Rob Jensen and his family, it offers a friendly, welcoming space for kids of all ages to learn and grow artistically. Recognized by various media outlets, Art for Kids Hub provides a diverse range of resources, including an engaging website, an online shop, and social media content full of art lessons. This platform is committed to making learning art fun and accessible, showcasing that art can be a delightful experience for everyone. It complements traditional art teaching by adding its unique, family oriented touch. Visit artforkidshub.com.

SOME WORDS OF GRATITUDE

In the creation of this book, I've been surrounded by an incredible circle of support and inspiration, each person contributing uniquely to this journey.

To Teryn, my wife and partner in everything: Your love, support, and friendship are the cornerstones of not only this book but of all our endeavors. I am endlessly grateful for your presence in my life. You make everything possible.

My deepest gratitude also goes to our children—Jack, Hadley, Austin, and Olivia. Your creativity, laughter, and shared joy in art have been the foundation of not only this book but all we do at Art for Kids Hub. You are my heart and inspiration.

A heartfelt thank you to DK, my publisher, for believing in this project. Pete Jorgensen, who first reached out to me with this wonderful opportunity: Your confidence in my work has been a great honor. Working with DK has been an enriching and fulfilling experience.

Special appreciation goes to Rebecca Razo and Elizabeth Gilbert at Coffee Cup Creative, LLC. Your expertise and vision have been instrumental in bringing this book to life. Your dedication and skill have transformed my ideas into something tangible and beautiful.

To my parents, Greg and Ruth Jensen, thank you for your unwavering encouragement and support since my childhood. Your belief in my passion for drawing has been a guiding light throughout my life and career.

I am also profoundly grateful to the young artists and their families who have joined us on Art for Kids Hub. Your enthusiasm and creativity have been a continuous source of inspiration and joy.

To the broader community of educators, fellow artists, and supporters, thank you for your encouragement and invaluable feedback. You have helped foster a nurturing space for young artists to thrive.

This book is a tribute to all of you. Your support, in so many ways, has made this journey an enriching and joyous adventure. Thank you for being part of our art family!